Exploring Christian Ethics Through Art

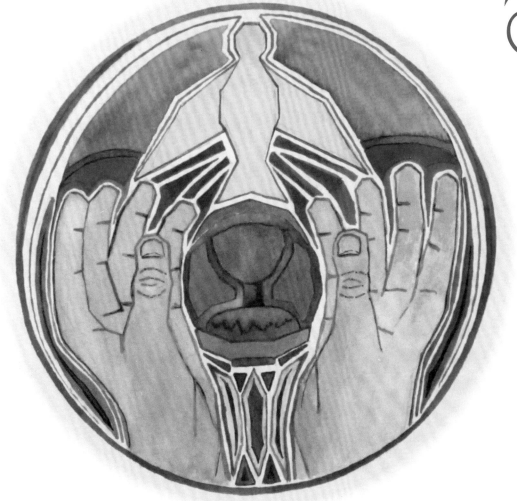

John H. Bower

McKnight
& Bishop
Inspire

ISBN 978-1-905691-11-1
A CIP catalogue record for this book is available from the British Library

First published in 2014 by McKnight & Bishop Inspire, an imprint of:

McKnight & Bishop Ltd.
28 Grifffiths Court,
Bowburn, Co. Durham, DH6 5FD
http://www.mcknightbishop.com
info@mcknightbishop .com

This books has been typeset in Palatino Linotype and Black Chancery

Contents

Foreword

Art has its own story to tell and often can be a means of telling another's story too, a picture can enhance the words of a poem, a story or a factual account. The words of scripture in the Bible convey the many facets of Christian faith in God and may bring to the reader's mind a picture of a truth that is being communicated.

A visual picture brings added interpretation of a Biblical text; an artist's own understanding is brought into play. Prayerful meditation plays its part and can give spiritual inspiration to the artist as they seek to interpret the story or teaching through the art they create.

The Bible holds a rich source of imagery when exploring the truths for living the Christian life. The artist can use this and then play a part in bringing the "Words of Life" alive to the beholder in an imaginative and inspirational way.

Through the pages of this book you are invited to read the texts and view the pictures presented and then through prayerful meditation allow yourself to be taken on a journey of discovery into the painting as you explore the facets of the picture and possibly see what the artist has seen and illustrated, but much more than that to be encouraged to see new nuances in the picture yourself which you alone have discovered as you interpret the text and find the truths that lay within. What stands out? What do you like or not like? Where do you see God in the picture?

The book starts at the beginning of the Church year with Advent leading up to the birth of Jesus, then continuing with His baptism, His temptation in the wilderness and the call of the disciples, The Sermon on the Mount, The Transfiguration, The healing at Bethesda, The feeding of the five thousand and the Pharisee and the Publican. The pictures then continue with the Easter theme starting with - The entry into Jerusalem and the cleansing of the Temple, The last supper, Jesus in The garden of Gethsemane, The Crucifixion of Christ, The Resurrection, The Ascension and The Holy Spirit's coming at Pentecost.

May the Holy Spirit guide you in your journey through this book. The aim is to enable you the explorer to deepen your faith and to find enrichment in your Christian walk through life.

God's richest blessing to you.

John H Bower -

Christ's Coming And Return

Luke 21:25-36

The Advent season brings to mind a time of waiting for the coming of Jesus into the world and also the promise of his second coming at the end of time.

Creation is in the pangs of continual change and the shadow of evil is always evident opposing the will and purpose of God.

People are caught up in the wild sea of life as the challenges and fears associated with the unknown prevail upon them.

God brings hope and the call to all people is to stand firm and put their trust in Jesus. Salvation is to be found through faith in Jesus.

In the passage the symbol of hope is the fig tree, its leaves appearing each year as a sign that the Kingdom of God is always near, ever present, always at hand.

EXPLORING THE PICTURE

> Can you see the contrasting light and darkness of the picture?
>
> Where do you see the turmoil and how do you interpret the dark side of the picture?
>
> Is there a partly concealed figure, a symbol of evil?
>
> Is there a falling away from grace conveyed in the picture, does this picture convey the majesty of God?
>
> The Son of Man is coming on a cloud with power and great glory.
>
> The people are standing firm and looking up, what is their expectation?
>
> How do you interpret the varying shapes and forms leading towards Jesus and also away from Jesus?
>
> Where can you see the road to life portrayed in the picture?
>
> Is the sun, shining so powerfully, a strange sign or a sign of the light that will always shine in the darkness?

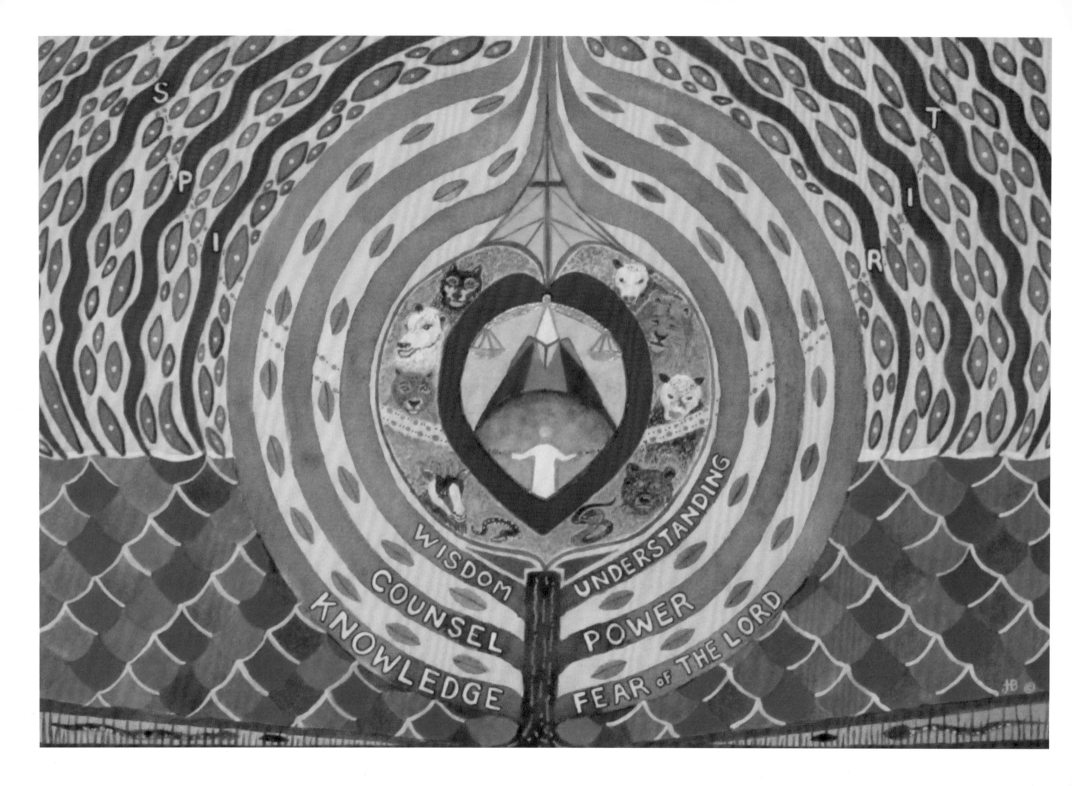

The Prophets

Isaiah 11:1-10

A message of hope coming out of new growth is the dominant theme in this passage.

A tree may be felled; however, if a stump remains there is always the possibility of new life.

The stump retains the DNA of the tree that once stood in its full glory.

Plants are pruned with the aim of promoting a more fruitful and wholesome growth.

Pruning to the uneducated may look destructive whereas in fact it is proved to be the best action that can be taken.

In regard to faith in God in what way can a remnant bring the opportunity for new growth?

Does the prophecy of Isaiah offer an optimistic and encouraging word?

The characteristics of God's chosen one are seen coming out of the stump.

Do these God given characteristics feature in today's society and in the world's priorities? If so how?

EXPLORING THE PICTURE

Jesus is at the heart of this picture.

Can you see the Spirit of God linking through the picture?

What does this prophesy have to say about harmony and peace?

The scales of justice symbolise equality for all.

What is the nature of the pruning that will bring about fairness into the lives of all people?

What other things in the picture lead you to further revelations?

John The Baptist

Luke 3:1-20

The scene is placed in its historical setting. The power takers and the rule makers are evident in the opening verses.

Into the life of ordinary people steps John the Baptist.

He brings God's call to people to repent and to symbolise their intent through baptism in the cleansing water of the Jordan River.

Change in lifestyle was the key theme of John's message; a new start he claimed was the only way back to God and a fulfilled life.

EXPLORING THE PICTURE

How do you interpret the picture?

Where are the markers of the Bible passage portrayed?

Where is the road that leads to God and who is portrayed as THE WAY?

Where is the source of the `Water of Life`

Why all the question marks and what are the questions raised in your mind?

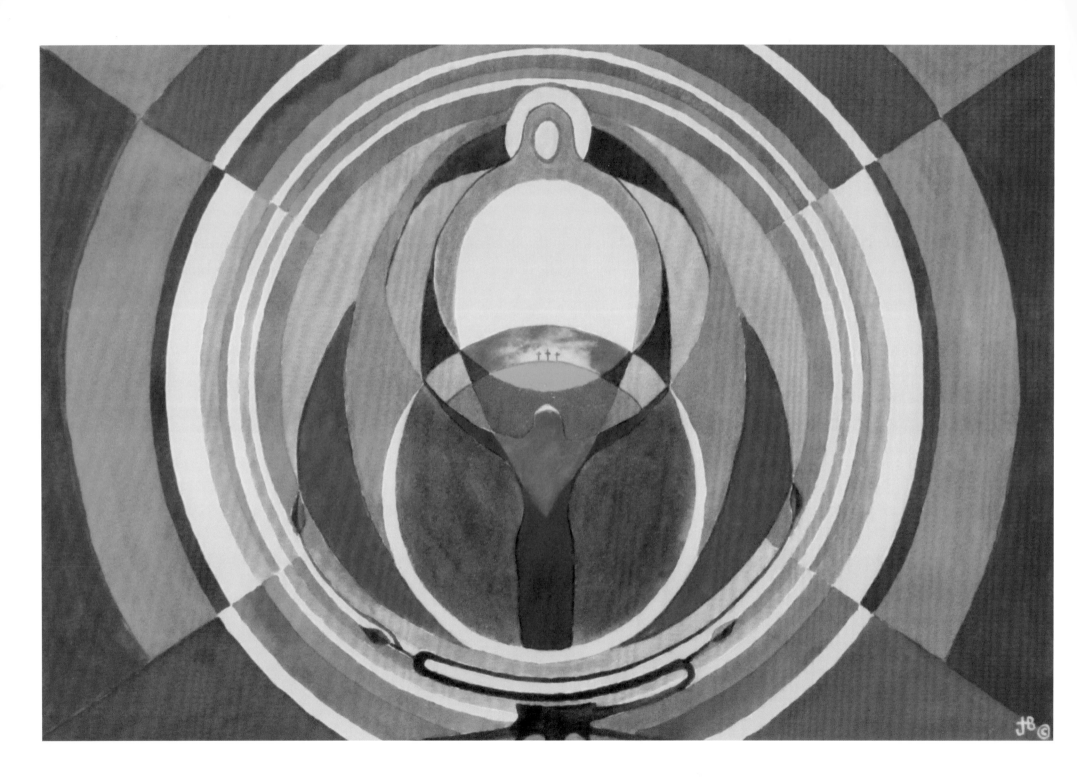

Mary

Luke 1:26-38

Do you think God was made vulnerable when Mary was asked to conceive Jesus?

Mary was very young and lived in the backwater town of Nazareth. She had no special status yet displayed great maturity and faith when asked to be the mother of Jesus.

Mary was mystified and uncomprehending yet gave her quiet acceptance of her calling with the words "I am the Lord's servant."

The conception of Jesus through the power of God's Holy Spirit challenges all human empires. It is mystery. It is an explosive story which remains controversial today.

EXPLORING THE PICTURE

Mary looks up, arms open wide to embrace God's call upon her.

What significance do the elliptical shapes have in relation to the Immaculate Conception?

Do you detect the root of Jesse which is a link back to the picture of the Prophets?

Can you see in the overlapping shapes, with reference to the divinity and humanity of Jesus?

Your eyes may fall on the crosses and all the cross has to convey of the purpose behind the birth of Jesus.

The power of God radiates from the centre, bursting with warmth and love and life.

There is also the cold colour blue a reminder that the dark presence of evil is ever present to challenge the goodness of God.

The Birth of Jesus

Luke 2 : 1 – 7

The concept of the incarnation brings the mind bending reality of God's entry into his world through the birth of Jesus.

The emphasis of the picture is the focussing of God's presence in the universe brought down to earth through the life of one vulnerable baby.

The birth of Jesus took place at God's chosen point in time and his birth came at a time when the world was dominated by earthly powers.

His birth had been foretold by the Prophets and now in God's time it had come to pass and the world would never be the same again.

EXPLORING THE PICTURE

There are a number of ways in which the focus of God's presence is illustrated. Can you see the way in which these have been included in the picture?

Can you see in the picture both the manner of Jesus' entry into the world and the manner of his leaving it?

There are signs of the road the believer can take to enter the Kingdom. The road is taken through faith in Jesus but what does the cross convey about the way the road has to be travelled?

What meaning do the red imposing arrows either side of the nativity scene convey to you?

What do the clouds above and the converging lines below the nativity scene represent to you?

Can you find other elements within the picture that relate to the way in which, at the incarnation, there was a meeting of heaven and earth?

The Baptism Of Jesus

Matthew 3:13-17

The Prophecy of Isaiah was fulfilled.

The message was pertinent.

The time was right.

The messenger was chosen a man down to earth in His simplicity and dedication.

The call and invitation was extended.

The warning of Judgement was evident.

Jesus insisted that John the Baptist should play his part in the fulfilment of the prophecy.

The event was momentous when God's presence was felt, when the focus of his power fell upon Jesus in the form of a dove and the acclamation was made "THIS IS MY BELOVED SON."

EXPLORING THE PICTURE

The colour, richness, variety and complexity of the moment are symbolic of God's omniscience, omnipresence, and omnipotence.

What kind of atmosphere is created within the picture?

Where does the image of the dove point and what does this convey to you?

What shapes and forms are created by the pattern within the painting and what does this say to you about the presence of God in the world?

The Temptation Of Jesus

Matthew 4:1-11

There is a focus on aloneness and the way fasting brought Jesus to the point of physical, mental and spiritual challenge and eventually to his discernment about his calling by God.

First the needs of the body brought the temptation of turning stones into bread.

Secondly Jesus needed mental clarity to ask the questions. 'Who am I, why am I here?' This brought Jesus to consider his own worth and personal importance and influence. He was tempted in his thoughts to test God. One way could be by throwing himself off the Temple, a temptation he resisted.

Thirdly there was the Spiritual struggle. Who was he to follow, who was to be his master?

He rejected the ways of the world in obedience to the ways of God. For him there could be no other possible way to achieve the salvation of the world. All other options would only perpetuate what already existed in the world, in the minds of human kind who rejected God.

EXPLORING THE PICTURE

Three distinct temptations reflected the power struggle for Jesus between following God's will over and against the diametrically opposite ways of the world in particular the evil instigated by the devil.

The picture illustrates the stones that could be turned into bread to feed millions. On the right the temple and the symbols of Jewish hierarchy, a lone figure is suspended in the air as in the mind of Jesus was planted the thought of testing God's willingness to save him from harm. To the left are the symbols of Roman and Jewish power in the world of that day, a power that could be at the disposal of Jesus if only he would submit to the devils ways. Unlimited human power is illustrated by a crown and countless riches. The overarching presence of God seen by the hands of God as the Holy Spirit's presence is brought to earth through God's promise. The shadow of crucifixion is ever present but there too is the hope for the world through resurrection.

Which part of the picture appeals to you?

Does any part of the picture relate to the temptations that draw you away from God's will?

The Call Of The Disciples

Mark 1:16-20

The call to repentance brought people face to face with their lack of obedience to God.

It brought them to a point of important decisions and to ask the question were they to carry on the lifestyle they now lived or were they going to turn their lives around and follow Jesus?

It was the question posed in the minds of four fishermen. We know their response.

It is, however, a call to every single person, in every age and generation, the call to follow Jesus.

True repentance is a complete turn around in life, not going the way of personal choice but going the way God chooses and directs.

It is the decision that leads to personal salvation, which in turn can lead to the Salvation of other people.

EXPLORING THE PICTURE

How does the picture draw you in and where is the central focus?

Do you get the feeling of the magnetism of the presence of Jesus expressed by the elliptical flow of line?

What does the right hand of Jesus indicate in its motion? Do you hear the call?

With the call goes the challenge "Take up your cross and follow me."

What does the light of the sun convey to you?

The Sermon On The Mount

Matthew Chapters 5-7

The people came from far and near to be with Jesus and to receive His response to their needs.

Disciples and multitude alike were captivated by the charismatic nature of Jesus who compelled them by his personality to make a response that was intended to draw them into his radically different world of God centred living - The Kingdom of God.

He met people's bodily, mental and spiritual needs and it was often in that order. People recognised their need of Him as they were embraced by the compassion of Jesus.

On the famous Sermon on the Mount Jesus reached beyond the physical to convey the real depths of true wholeness which he offered and showed people how they too could live the Kingdom life.

The many facets of the Kingdom were revealed and displayed through healing, through teaching and through meeting the inner spiritual and life fulfilling needs.

EXPLORING THE PICTURE

The all encompassing nature of the picture puts Jesus at the centre and everyone concentred around him.

Each person is held in relationship – first with Jesus then with each other.

Do you see any distinction between the people's positions in the picture?

Are some people closer to Jesus by choice or could there be a spiritual interpretation of their position?

What does the picture say to you about the proclamation of Jesus' teaching?

All people are equal and all have access to Jesus, all are invited into The Kingdom.

What other aspects of the picture speak to you?

How does the picture and the text invite you to Kingdom living?

The Transfiguration Of Jesus

Luke 9:28-36

The three disciples were called to witness the Transfiguration of Jesus and later, after the resurrection, would bring their own witness to enlighten all believers thereafter.

The symbolic choice of the mountain, the quiet majesty of the setting, was to be the ideal location for the Transfiguration. The two great leaders of former years – Moses and Elijah reaffirmed the prophetic message and the place of Jesus in God's Kingdom.

The three disciples witnessed 'the Glory' of Jesus and heard God the Father's confirmation of Jesus' relationship within the Godhead. Fear and awe were the experience of the disciples. Jesus commanded their silence about what they had witnessed and they themselves so taken with the seemingly unbelievable event were not to speak about it until after the rising of Jesus from the dead.

EXPLORING THE PICTURE

Observe the awesome scene where the rocky mountain top adds drama to the Transfiguration event.

Do the disciples seem dwarfed by the figures of Jesus, Moses and Elijah? What does this convey to you?

The cloud hovers overhead waiting to cast a mystery over the scene is this often true of life?

Close your eyes and imagine the scene filled with the glorious presence of God.

Healing At Bethesda

John 5:1-9

The Pool of Bethesda which was near the Sheep gate was where a large number of invalids – the blind, the lame and the paralysed congregated in the desperate hope of a cure from their infirmities. The water had healing properties when it was in flux.

There was one man who had been ill for 38 years. In 38 years he had never made it he needed to be first in for the cure to take place.

Jesus asked him the question "Do you want to be healed?"

Then He commanded him "Rise take up your bed and walk" he did, he was healed.

This is only one of countless healings performed by Jesus – some recorded in the other Gospels too but many not recorded and therefore lost to us.   Never-the-less there are enough to bring the realisation that the healing power of Jesus was used in many different ways for different conditions all with the one aim to meet individual needs and to bring them freedom from their illness and wholeness to their life.

EXPLORING THE PICTURE

The picture focuses upon Jesus and the individual and personal approach He makes to the man.

How are time and movement illustrated, before, during and after the healing?

Imagine in this freeze frame mode you are able to move forward with the man towards Jesus. What would you say to Jesus?

The man is laying on the pallet as Jesus approaches him, then during his healing he rises up, grows in stature and then fully upright is face to face and eye to eye and toe to toe with Jesus his wholeness is completed through the healing power of Jesus.

What can you see in the background that is the symbol of salvation?

Feeding The Five Thousand

John 6:1-14

Jesus attracted great crowds of people everyone with their own motives for seeking Him out. Jesus felt it important to provide for the people's physical needs as well as their mental and spiritual needs.

The small amount of food was transformed into much when placed into the hands of Jesus.   Could it be said there was then and is now always more than enough to provide for people's needs when sharing takes place?

The Grace of God is always in evidence.   Often the willingness of people's own giving of themselves and their willingness to be available in service to Jesus is lacking.

The boy provides a symbolic focus for what it means to give ALL to Jesus, even one person can be effective in the service of the Kingdom and be a partner in God's plan to bring all people to a life of wholeness.

EXPLORING THE PICTURE

What is portrayed both physically and spiritually through the open hand of Jesus?

There is the hint of the Sea of Tiberius, the green grass of the hills, Andrew and the boy.

What is conveyed by the overarching sky, the flowing fields, do they pay homage to the unity and harmony of creation?

What else can you see in the scene that is pictured?

The Phairsee And The Tax Collector (Prayer)

Luke 18:9-14

The Parable of the Pharisee and the Tax Collector focuses upon prayer and the right way to approach God.

Prayer can bring an individual into the presence of God.

No one has any cause to be puffed up with pride for whatever reason for before God no one measures up to Christ.

Humility is the key and through a humble approach to God then each person can be drawn in to greater awareness of the promise of God in each and every area and experience of life.

EXPLORING THE PICTURE

The Pharisee and the Tax Collector stand apart, one sure of his own importance and religious correctness, the other conscious of his many failings and his desire to be right with God.

Can you see the jewel of hope dropping into this scene and into the Tax Collector's act of repentance is full of light, sourced from God's acceptance of him?

Jesus stands within the scene do you detect the Holy Spirit's presence bringing the Tax Collector the forgiveness he so longs for?

Behind the Pharisee the colours are drab and dark a sign of a misguided approach to God.

Behind the Tax Collector the colours are vivid and bright a sign of the way to God through humility of heart.

At the left hand of Jesus is a space waiting to be filled, by whom do you think?

Entry Into Jerusalem & Cleansing The Temple

Matthew 21:1-22 & Luke 19:29-48

Within the account of the Entry into Jerusalem and the Cleansing of the Temple lies both acclaim and accusation – rejoicing and judgement. The expectation of the coming of the Messiah was looked forward to by many but not all. The claim that Jesus was the Messiah was not universally accepted. For many Jesus' claim rang true. For the sceptics Jesus did not fit in with their idea of who the Messiah should be like. Jesus challenges world views and worldly lifestyle.

The Cleansing of the Temple brought into question the whole style of religious life and interpretation of God's law. Jesus criticised the focus of Jewish Religion and how the true worship of God had become sidelined in the interests of human self aggrandisement and material gain.

EXPLORING THE PICTURE

At the centre of the picture Jesus is surrounded by the crowds as He enters Jerusalem riding on a colt, the cloaks and palms spread out before Him.

Can you see the reference to the Kingship of Jesus in the picture?

Can you see the weeping eye? (Luke 19:41)

In the Temple what does the overturned tables of the money changers signal about the judgement of God?

Where are the words of Matthew 21:21-22 depicted in the picture?

How do you interpret the right hand side of the picture, what do the arched colours convey to you in relation to Holy Week?

What else can you see in the picture?

The Last Supper

Matthew 26:17-29, Mark 14:12-25, Luke 22: 14-20 (21-38), John 18:1-30.

The Last Supper gives us an insight into the intimate relationship of Jesus and his disciples.

Jesus had made detailed preparations for that night. Nothing had been left to chance. Everything was in place for Him to bring a personal word to each one gathered in the upper room.

This special gathering brought within it new meaning to the traditional meal of the Passover which forever would be associated with Christian Liturgy for all time.

The everyday elements of bread and wine were to be forever associated with the Body and Blood of Christ, symbolic of His indwelling life, through the presence of the Holy Spirit in all believers.

EXPLORING THE PICTURE:

Jesus has central place around the table, where do you see the presence of the Holy Spirit?

What does the part of the picture above and below the central line convey to you?

Can you see where the inverted arch of God's presence reaches down and is focussed on the Bread and Wine?

Where do you see the offer of life flowing out from the goblet towards the disciples and the world?

Each disciple is linked in the circle of the table what does this linking convey to you about their relationship?

What other elements within the painting speak to you?

The Garden Of Gethsemane

Matthew 26:36-46

This is one of the most poignant pictures portrayed through the words of the Gospels and ranks only second to the account of the Crucifixion
in its portrayal of the pain and anguish of Jesus.

It depicts the loneliness of Jesus and his spiritual and mental struggle with the temptation to turn away from God's will.

Jesus' earthly ministry was being drawn towards its conclusion.

The questions that were raised for Jesus in that present moment of time would determine whether the salvation of the world would be accomplished through him.

EXPLORING THE PICTURE

All human presence has been excluded from the picture in order that Jesus is central.

Jesus lays prostrate on the craggy rocks praying to His father that the dreadful time of a painful death might be taken away from Him.

Can you sense the oppressive scene as the trees hideously and threateningly enfold Jesus and convey the dreadful weight of what lies ahead?

The darkness and bleakness of the scene symbolises the evil opposing Jesus in every possible way. How do you recognise the opposition and evil in your life?

The Spirit of God reaches down through the blackness to enfold Jesus as if with protective arms.

The image suspends time and emphasises the loneliness of Jesus who is without any human support.

All his strength comes from God the Father and the Holy Spirit.

The Crucifixion Of Jesus

Mark 15:21-39.

The accounts in the four Gospels bring together all the elements of the last earth bound day of Jesus.

They capture the stark reality of the way Jesus stood out, stood alone and stood up against the forces of evil.

At Golgotha, among the crowds, where those who were determined to see the death of Jesus and those who longed for his release.

Many people have died for a cause, many have died to defend another, and many have died who have been innocent of any offence.

Jesus died choosing through his death to offer the world the God given gift of true life leading to eternal life.

EXPLORING THE PICTURE

Jesus is the central focus of the scene.

Where do you see the symbolism of those things that mark the death of Jesus?

See the crown of thorns within the scene at Golgotha. Reflect on the dark influence of evil that comes through.

Consider the contrast between the darkness within the picture and the light that radiates out from Jesus.

The larger than life nails convey an overwhelming force threatening to engulf and oppress Jesus.

The drops of red blood point to the humanity of Jesus and to his sacrificial death on the cross but also symbolise the salvation of the world brought through his death.

When you think about the eclipse of the sun and the moment when the light to the world was temporally removed, what spiritual understanding do you think lies within this natural occurrence?

Below the 'Cross of Christ' is the path that leads from Christ and to the offer God makes through Christ of a new life for all people.

The Resurrection Of Jesus

John 20:1-10, Luke 24:1-12, Mark 16:1-8, Matthew 28:1-10

The mystery of the Resurrection will always remain.

It relies for its confirmation not on scientific forensic evidence but on the faith of the believer.

The Power of God which brought the universe into being and created the world is the same power that raised Jesus from the dead.

The Power of God is at work in the world today. It is as possible to explain away the Resurrection as it is to explain away many other events and happenings in the world that appear mysterious.

The experience of changed lives and circumstances are proof of something beyond the human ability to explain.

Human Spirituality leads us into another dimension of awareness, to something above and beyond the physical and material. God communicates with human beings in such a way that the whole perspective and understanding of life can display the new world God wants everyone to share in – this is "The Kingdom of God."

EXPLORING THE PICTURE

The darkened tomb is hedged in on either side by dark colours of death and despair fighting to keep Jesus locked in the tomb and hidden.

Can you sense the power of God bursting upwards and outwards from the Tomb's centre?

The power breaks through the tombs façade and core. The cross is held in limbo in the light and becomes a light itself.

How can the picture be interpreted within the content of its elements?

Where does the shadow of Christ's figure feature?

What more can you see in the picture?

The Ascension Of Jesus

Matthew 28:16-20.

The Ascension of Jesus brought awe and wonder to those who witnessed it. Standing before Peter, James and John was the visible presence of the risen Jesus. This was to be his last appearance, the final assurance that he had been raised from death.

It was to be more than that. It was to be the time of the great commission to be acted upon by them and others and for future generations to come. Jesus command was "Go into all the world and make disciples of all people, baptizing them in the name of the Father, the Son, and the Holy Spirit.

It was to be a visual departure but not an absence of Christ's presence in the world for Jesus went on to say, "I am with you always even to the end of the age." (Matthew 28:20b) The promise of the Holy Spirit was to be laid upon their hearts and minds. They were from that moment to wait upon the Lord.

EXLORING THE PICTURE

The picture's aim is to depict the risen Christ ascending to the Godhead.

The light is symbolic of Jesus' divinity embracing the rainbow colours recognising the many facets of the Holy Spirit.

The shaping of Jesus' ascent signifies his breaking through from the earth into heaven.

From the visible life he lived among people into the physically invisible life within the Spiritual realm of God.

Footnote:

Though this picture was painted to symbolically represent the Ascension of Jesus, by turning the picture 180 degrees the picture can be an illustration of the coming of the Holy Spirit on the day of Pentecost.

The Holy Spirit

Acts 2:1-21.

The complexity of the picture on the one hand conveys symbolically the mystery of God and on the other hand the order shape and design within God's creation and the spiritual realm.

Above all, within all, and through all is GOD.

The coming of the Holy Spirit on the day of Pentecost marked the Birth of the Church. Thereafter many accounts were written and spoken about which conveyed the power of the Holy Spirit in the life of the individual, the Church and the world.

God is omnipresent, omniscient and omnipotent.

EXPLORING THE PICTURE

What can you see within the picture?

What does the centre of the picture say to you?

At the heart of the picture is a reminder of the cross on which Jesus died for all, a reminder of His love for the world.

The hands of Christ enfold the one who is praying, embracing the person in that love of God.

Is a life open to God's Spirit able to deepen relationship, to answer need and to receive direction for living a life that is Christ-centred?

Do you observe the flames of the Holy Spirit what does this prompt you to recall in relationship to the Holy Spirit?

The concentric circles are a reminder of the all embracing love of God.

Can you observe the doves? What do they convey to you?

The multiple shapes and colours are a reminder of the many facets of God's character.

May the Holy Spirit guide you and lead you closer to God.

About The Artist

John Hardcastle Bower was born in Richmond North Yorkshire but spent all of his childhood and early adulthood in Darlington. Painting has always been something he has engaged in from his schooldays. His Christian faith grew out of those early days and later this was expressed through youth work and especially as a Captain in The Boys' Brigade in his home church: Northland Methodist.

He felt a call to the Methodist Ministry in his late forties and after training in Manchester this was followed by ordination at the Methodist church in Cullercoats. He has served in Methodist circuit churches in Sheffield South and Leicester West and as Superintendent Minister in the Spennymoor & Ferryhill Circuit in county Durham.

John is married to Margaret. They have one son Andrew who is married to Sandra and they have two grandchildren, Kate and Alfie. He is now a Supernumerary minister in the Darlington Circuit.

John's other hobbies are wood turning and wood carving which blend aptly with his creative bent. John endeavours to use his gift of art as one way of illustrating and expressing his faith in God. He realises that faith is a mammoth and impossible task to convey completely through the media of art. Yet the challenge is hard to resist and hopefully the journey will bring rewards, not only to him but also to those who take the journey for themselves.

John's wife Margaret suffers from a neurological movement disorder and all the profits from the sale of this book will go to support the work and research of this charity.

About The Publisher

McKnight & Bishop are always on the lookout for great new authors and ideas for exciting new books. If you write or if you have an idea for a book, email us: **info@mcknighbishop.com** Some things we love are: undiscovered authors, open-source software, crowd-funding, Amazon/Kindle, social networking, faith, laughter and new ideas.